Be b

This book belongs to

_____

Written by Stephen Barnett
Illustrated by Rosie Brooks

Contents

Be brave 3

Cheating never works 13

A good deed everyday 21

New words 31

What did you learn? 32

About this book

This book teaches children how to be brave in the dark, never to cheat and to do a good deed everyday. Questions in the end helps to test the child's attention, and the section on new words encourages vocabulary building.

Be brave

We can all get a little bit scared of things every now and then. We worry more when we are alone.

Many a time, we are frightened of a test we have to appear for in school . . .

. . . or we are scared of a strange, unknown noise at night when we're lying alone in bed in the darkness.

Most of the things that we worry about, do not happen. We are more frightened about what we think might happen. Think about how you can overcome your fears.

If you have studied hard for a test at school, then you have done your best. Stop worrying about the marks you will get. Try to do the test well.

Be brave. If you don't do well in the test, study harder for the next one. Try to work on your mistakes the next time.

Sometimes you might hear noises at night. It may be the wind pushing a branch against your window or a cat scratching on your door.

Be brave. Turn on your light and look around. You may call your parents if needed.

Be brave! You will feel much better after you have overcome your fear.

Cheating never works

It was my final test at school that day. When I saw the test paper, my heart sank! There were many questions the answers of which I didn't know!

I didn't know what to do as I didn't want to get low marks. I thought, 'Perhaps I can copy a few answers from someone else's paper!'

I looked into my friend's paper. I knew that he had studied hard and would do well in the test.

Finally, the test came to an end and we handed our papers to our teacher. As the children left the classroom, the teacher asked me to stay back.

'I was checking the test papers. I think you need to explain a few things to me. Your answers are the same as Robert's!' said my teacher.

'Did you copy this from Robert?' the teacher asked me. 'Yes,' I said. 'I'm sorry.' 'It is unfair to cheat like this, Kevin. You are only cheating yourself!'

'I want you to study hard tonight at home and take this test again tomorrow,' she said. The next day, I did the test quite well without cheating.

A good deed everyday

My grandmother used to say that we should all do a good deed everyday no matter how small it is. This would make a lot of difference to us.

It could be a kind word to someone who is feeling sad . . .

. . . or maybe giving water to a thirsty animal on a hot day.

'When you do something like this you are passing along goodness,' my grandmother said. 'You are giving something without asking for any return. This makes it even better!'

It was a weekend. I was outside after breakfast when I heard a mewing sound. My neighbour's kitten was stuck way up on a tree.

I quickly went inside the house to get a stool. I wanted to bring down the poor kitten.

I stood on the stool and reached up to the branch where the kitten was. I carefully lifted it down and gave it to Mr. Williams, our neighbour.

'That was very kind of you dear,' said
Mr. Williams. 'Thank you!' I felt so good.

'Your good deed for the day,' said my father smiling happily at me.

New words

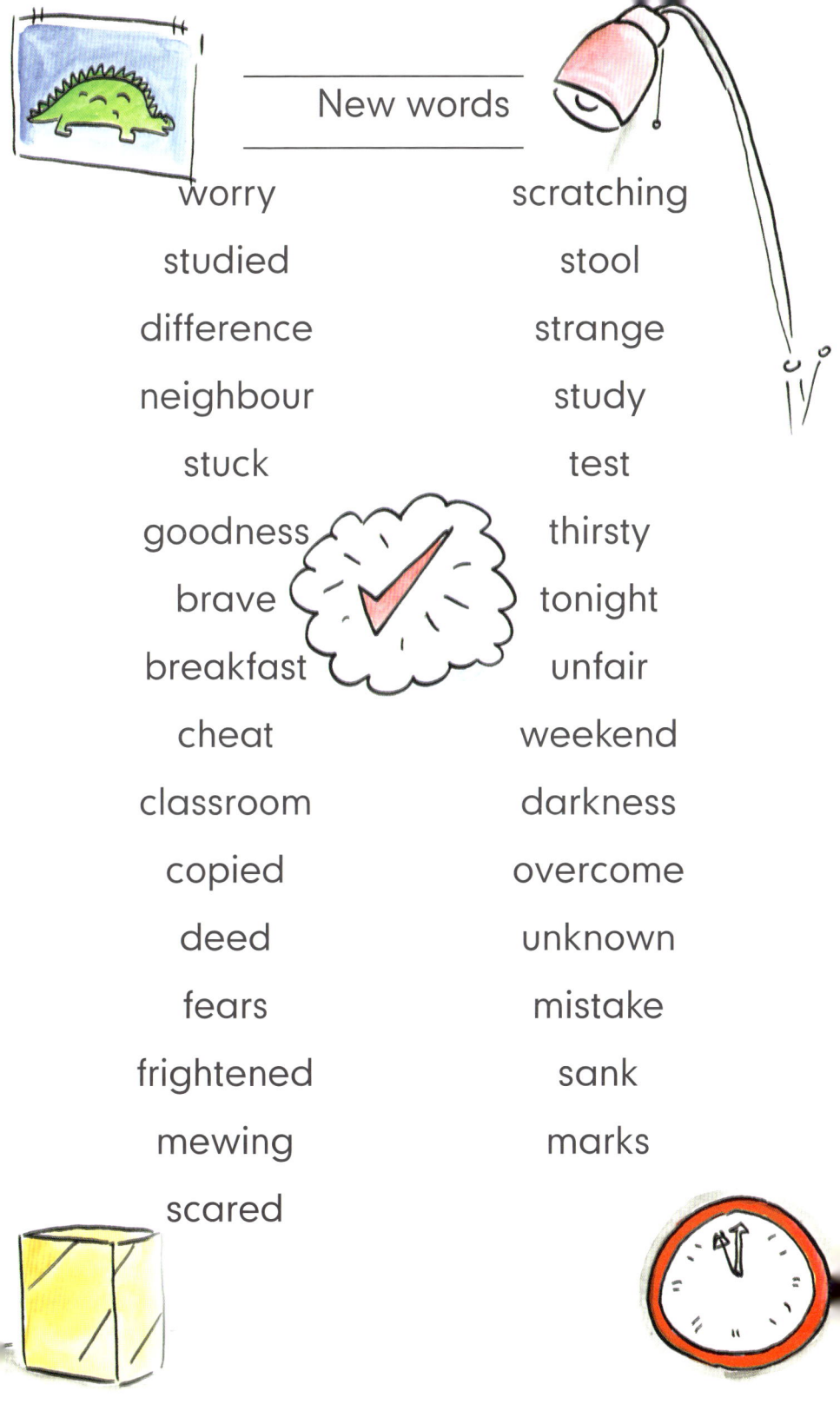

worry	scratching
studied	stool
difference	strange
neighbour	study
stuck	test
goodness	thirsty
brave	tonight
breakfast	unfair
cheat	weekend
classroom	darkness
copied	overcome
deed	unknown
fears	mistake
frightened	sank
mewing	marks
scared	

What did you learn?

Be brave
How can you be brave?
What should you do when you are afraid?

Cheating never works
Why did the child cheat?
What did the teacher ask Kevin?

A good deed everyday
What good deed did the child do?
What was stuck up on a tree?
What was the neighbour's name?